DOV DOV AND THE MAN WHO FORGOT
and other stories

by Yona Weinberg

illustrated by Liat Benyaminy Ariel

FIRST EDITION
First Impression . . . September, 1991

Published and Distributed by
MESORAH PUBLICATIONS, Ltd.
Brooklyn, New York 11232

Distributed in Israel by
MESORAH MAFITZIM / J. GROSSMAN
Rechov Harav Uziel 117
Jerusalem, Israel

Distributed in Australia & New Zealand by
GOLD'S BOOK & GIFT CO.
36 William Street
Balaclava 3183, Vic., Australia

Distributed in Europe by
J. LEHMANN HEBREW BOOKSELLERS
20 Cambridge Terrace
Gateshead, Tyne and Wear
England NE8 1RP

Distributed in South Africa by
KOLLEL BOOKSHOP
22 Muller Street
Yeoville 2198
Johannesburg, South Africa

ARTSCROLL YOUTH SERIES®
DOV DOV AND THE MAN WHO FORGOT AND OTHER STORIES
© Copyright 1991, by YONA WEINBERG and MESORAH PUBLICATIONS, Ltd.
4401 Second Avenue / Brooklyn, N.Y. 11232 / (718) 921-9000

ALL RIGHTS RESERVED.

No part of this book may be reproduced
in any form — including photocopying and retrieval systems —
without **written** permission from the copyright holder,
except by a reviewer who wishes to quote brief passages in connection with a review
written for inclusion in magazines or newspapers.

THE RIGHTS OF THE COPYRIGHT HOLDER WILL BE STRICTLY ENFORCED.

ISBN:
0-89906-974-6 (hard cover)
0-89906-999-1 (paperback)

Typography by CompuScribe at ArtScroll Studios, Ltd.
4401 Second Avenue / Brooklyn, N.Y. 11232 / (718) 921-9000

Printed in the United States of America by
EDISON LITHOGRAPHING AND PRINTING CORP.
Bound by Sefercraft, Quality Bookbinders, Ltd. Brooklyn, N.Y.

מסורה

ArtScroll Youth Series®

AUTHOR: Weinberg, Yona
TITLE: Dov Dov & the Man who Forgot & Other Stories

DATE LOANED	BORROWER'S NAME
12/4	Avi W Rm 20

Dov Dov & the Man Who Forgot & Other Stories

A Dov Dov Book

Table of Contents

Dov Dov and the Man Who Forgot 7

Flight to New York 14

Mine Very Own Homon 22

The Wild Stallion 30

The Skunk Hero 36

Go Ahead and Shoot Me 44

The Old Man 50

Opening Night 54

Dov Dov and the Big Potch 59

Dov Dov and the Man Who Forgot

Dov Dov walked in the door, turned on the light, and screamed.

"What happened?" His father came running. "Oh no! You turned on the light."

Dov Dov stood with his hand covering his open mouth. "I forgot," he whispered.

It was *Shabbos* and this was the third time Dov Dov had forgotten and turned on the light on *Shabbos*.

"Why didn't you put tape on the light switch before *Shabbos*?" his father asked.

"I forgot," Dov Dov repeated. It seemed he kept forgetting these things, over and over again.

"Dov Dov, come into the study with me."

Dov Dov followed his father. What was his father going to do? It wasn't his fault he'd turned on the light. He just kept forgetting. It was an accident. That's all.

Dov Dov's father closed the study door and motioned to Dov Dov to have a seat beside him.

"Dov Dov, did you eat today?"

"Of course! I had *cholent* and chicken and *kishka* and chocolate pie."

"Good!" His father paused. "Who won the ball game yesterday?" he asked.

Dov Dov was puzzled. Why was his father changing the subject? "We did."

"Good! You were there?"

"Sure! I always go to the game!"

"Now, I think it's time I told you a little story about a friend of mine."

A story? Was that all? Dov Dov made himself comfortable and listened to his father's story:

❈ ❈ ❈

A long time ago, when I was still a teenager in the *yeshivah*, a very strange thing happened. Reb Gershon, who worked downtown, came home after a hard day's work. He parked his car, got out, and walked up his driveway.

"Reb Gershon!" called his neighbor, "What is the matter? Is everything O.K?"

"What do you mean?" Reb Gershon asked.

The neighbor looked as if he had seen a ghost. "What's wrong? What happened?" he yelled.

"What do you mean?" Reb Gershon repeated.

The neighbor looked at him with disbelief. "How come you were driving today? It's *Shavuos*! Did you take someone to the hospital?" he asked.

Reb Gershon's face turned white. His knees began to shake. "*Shavuos*! Oh, my goodness! I forgot!" The words left his mouth in a painful sigh.

"You forgot!?"

Reb Gershon went into his house and collapsed in a chair. "What have I done?" he moaned. "How could I forget that today is *Shavuos*, the time when we received the *Torah*?"

He paced back and forth in his living room, moaning and shaking his head. How could he forget such an important day?

How could he not remember that it was *Yom Tov?*

He took his hat and left the house. He walked with his head down, his hands in his pockets. He shook his head over and over again and trembled in shock.

The *Rosh Yeshivah* would know what he should do. Yes! That's where he would go. The *Rosh Yeshivah* would tell him what to do to erase this terrible mistake.

"Come in!" The *Rosh Yeshivah* smiled when he saw Reb Gershon.

Reb Gershon walked in, downcast and miserable. He told the *Rosh Yeshivah* about the strange thing that had happened to him. The *Rosh Yeshivah* shook his head sadly. He thought for a while. Then, he spoke.

"Reb Gershon, there is only one thing I can suggest for you to do."

"What is it? I'll do anything!" said the miserable man.

The *Rosh Yeshivah* said, "You must quit your job and become a *shammas* in a *shul*."

"A what?"

"A *shammas*. The man who takes care of the *shul*! Only then will such a thing never happen to you again. If you are a *shammas* in a *shul*, you will never forget when it is *Shabbos* or *Yom Tov*."

The *Rosh Yeshivah* looked at him with kind eyes. "When something is important enough to you," he said, "you don't forget it. Does anyone forget his wedding day? *Shabbos* and *mitzvos* should be more important to you than anything else in the world because they were given to us by *Hashem*."

Reb Gershon thanked the *Rosh Yeshivah* and tried to follow his advice. There was one problem. Every *shul* that he went to already had a *shammas* and did not need him.

Dov Dov and the Man Who Forgot

Again and again, Reb Gershon heard the same words. He was desperate.

"I'll tell you what I'll do," he said to one *shammas*. "I'll do all of your work and you can just stay home; I'll give you the money

that I earn."

But, no! No *shammas* was willing to give up his job. Reb Gershon tried again and again, but to no avail. Finally, he had only one choice left, and that is what he did.

Reb Gershon started his own *shul* and became its *shammas*. Every day, he was the first to arrive at *shul*. He straightened the benches, stacked the *sefarim*, and washed the floors.

The *shul* became Reb Gershon's life. He loved it and treasured it as a jeweler does a precious stone. Every *Shabbos* and *Erev Yom Tov* he took special pride in the care he put into the holy building as he polished and scrubbed.

On Fridays he removed each *Sefer Torah* tenderly to check it and rolled the parchment to the right *sidrah* of the week before placing it back in the *Aron Kodesh*.

Before *Rosh Hashanah* he replaced the blue velvet *paroches* covering the *Aron Kodesh* with a fresh, clean white one.

Each year, when *Shavuos* came around, Reb Gershon put extra effort into his work as he decorated the *shul* with fresh flowers and pine ferns that he cut from his own garden.

Years passed and Reb Gershon never forgot his *Rosh Yeshivah's* words. "When something is important enough to you, you don't forget it."

❁ ❁ ❁

Dov Dov's father's story was finished. Dov Dov sat still, staring at his hands. If something is important to you, you don't forget it. Does he forget to eat? To play? What can be more important than doing *Hashem's* will?

"I understand, Abba," he said "I'm sorry! But what can I do to make sure I remember to tape the light switch before *Shabbos*?"

"How about making yourself some sign?" said his father. "When you look at it, you'll always remember what it's for. And leave the tape in a place where you will be sure to see it on Friday."

Dov Dov thought, "I've got it!" he shouted. And he did.

The next Friday afternoon, the boys called for Dov Dov for their weekly Friday afternoon ball game.

"I'm coming," called Dov Dov. He took his bat and joined his friends.

"Hey, Dov Dov! What's that stuck to your bat?"

"Oh, it's just some tape! Wait a minute, guys! I have something to do before we go!"

He trotted breathlessly home and ran up the stairs to his room, two steps at a time, carrying his baseball bat in one hand and a roll of masking tape in the other.

Flight to New York

Naomi felt a distinct thrill of pleasure as the plane took off. Zoom, zoom . . . faster and faster.

"Look, Goldie," said Naomi to her doll, as she held her close, and looked out of the window, "say goodbye to Bubby and Zeidy down there."

The wheels left the ground and the plane shot higher and higher. Through the window Naomi saw the houses and trees get smaller and smaller until they looked like little ants covering green hills. The clouds zoomed closer. Naomi watched as the plane crashed into the white clouds, soared above them, high into the blue skies.

"Mommy, how long will it be until we get home?"

"Oh, Mammele, it will be a long trip, but it was worth it, wasn't it?" Mrs. Katz said.

Mrs. Katz fixed two year old Avremele's seat belt tightly about him.

"It sure was fun," said Naomi enthusiastically. "It was great seeing Bubby and Zeidy and the *Kosel* and all the *shuls* and everything, but I'll be glad to get home again and sleep in my own bed."

Mrs. Katz smiled. "Yes, it was a wonderful three weeks but I'll be grateful when this long journey is over."

Naomi looked at the family sitting in front of her. A little boy about three years old, with peanut butter on his face, was peeking at her through the crack between the seats. Next to him sat a little girl, about a year younger, sucking on a bottle. The father was holding an infant and the mother had her hands full entertaining and feeding her youngsters.

An elderly couple sat across the aisle. The man had a grayish beard and was holding a *sefer*. The woman was looking into a *Tehillim*. She looked up, saw Naomi, and smiled. Naomi smiled back. The plane was full of noisy children, busy parents and busy stewardesses bringing food and drinks.

"Stay close to me, Goldie," Naomi said to her doll, "and I'll take good care of you. It's going to be a long trip."

The minutes seemed to drag into long hours. Naomi slept on and off. She felt thirsty and hungry.

"Mommy, can I have something to eat? Are we almost there?"

"The stewardess will give us some food soon, but it will still be a long time till we get home. In a little while we'll be landing for a short stop in Brussels for the plane to refuel."

"Where is Brussels?"

"It's in Belgium."

"Oh," said Naomi, "it sounds like a vegetable." She laughed. "How long are we going to be there?"

"Not long, hopefully."

"Have you ever been there, Mommy?"

"No, I haven't," she answered, as she gathered her belongings together.

It was 4:30 in the middle of the night when they arrived in Brussels.

"Are we going to get off the plane?" asked Naomi, yawning.

"I guess we can exercise our legs a bit, even though it's only for a short time."

At nine o'clock in the morning they heard the announcement.

"Attention all passengers. Attention all passengers," the loudspeaker boomed. "There will be a slight delay for minor repairs. Please wait for further announcements."

At eleven o'clock the departure was still being delayed.

"Mommy, when are we going to leave? I'm hungry." Naomi was getting scared.

"I don't know, but I hope it's soon. I'm running very short of milk and food for the baby."

Avremele squirmed in her arms as she tried to diaper him. By two o'clock in the afternoon special buses came to take the five hundred passengers to a nearby hotel.

"Mommy, what are we going to do? Is there enough food for us? Will there be kosher food in the hotel?" Naomi asked.

"I don't know. I sure hope so," said Mrs. Katz. Her voice was strained and dry. To her dismay, the airline used up all the food and drinks and there was still no word about when the repairs would be finished.

"I'm starving," Naomi began to cry as thoughts of going without food caused her stomach to growl.

"I know, Mammele." Mrs. Katz shook her head.

What were they going to do and where were all these people going now?

"Excuse me, Miss," said Mrs. Katz, "but where is everyone going?"

"Oh, thank goodness!" said the lady. "The airline is offering coupons for free meals in the airport restaurant." The lady laughed. "Thank goodness we won't starve."

Mrs. Katz turned white. "But, Mommy," Naomi began to cry, "the airport restaurant doesn't serve kosher food." She felt a terrible sinking feeling in her stomach. "Are we going to starve?"

"No, Mammele, we're not. Just be patient. *Daven*. Something will turn up soon. I'm sure."

Naomi saw the little boy who had been sitting in front of her.

"Mommy," he demanded, "I'm hungry. I want a cookie."

His little sister was holding her empty bottle and crying, "Botti! Botti!"

Naomi clutched her doll in her cold, trembling hands. "Don't cry," Naomi heard someone say. It was the elderly lady who had been sitting across the aisle from her. She looked pale and tired.

"But I'm hungry and scared," Naomi whined.

"Yes, dear, we all are, but I'm sure things will work out soon."

"But what if it takes forever to fix the plane? We can't go on forever without food."

The lady put her hand on Naomi's shoulder. "Forever is a long time, dear. Don't worry. I doubt we'll be here that long. I'm sure *Hashem* will send us help soon. We've got to have trust in Him."

"That's what my mother said too," Naomi said. "But it's hard to have trust when my stomach is grumbling so loudly."

"Yes," said the lady. "It's easier to have faith when our stomachs are full and we feel contented and safe."

"Here we are stuck in this foreign country," said Naomi. "We don't even know anyone here. It's a strange country, Belgium! We have nothing to eat and nothing to drink. Even Avremele doesn't have any baby food left. Oh! I wish I were home!"

Naomi's mother hugged her and repeated, "We have to have *bitachon* and faith. You'll see! Things will work out. Come on, wipe those tears away. Let's say a little *Tehillim* together."

"Goldie, don't be scared," Naomi whispered to her doll. "I'll take good care of you." She felt the wet hard cheek of her doll against her cheek, moist from her own tears. "*Hashem* will take care of us, Goldie. You'll see. 'We've got to have *bitachon*,'

Mommy said, and she knows. Stay close to me and I'll take good care of you."

Afternoon turned into evening. People were losing their patience. Naomi felt drowsy. She rested her head on her mother's shoulder. "Please, *Hashem,* send me some food. I'm so hungry."

Naomi slept a troubled, uncomfortable sleep. "Naomi, wake up! Wake up!"

Could this be a dream? Naomi thought she smelled something delicious. The aroma of freshly cooked dishes filled her nostrils. There in front of her were boxes and boxes of food, milk for the babies, fruits, bread, cake, and the mouth-watering aroma of lots and lots of tasty food.

"Mommy, am I dreaming or is this a miracle?" Naomi asked. "Did *Hashem* send *mohn* down to us?"

Mrs. Katz laughed. "Yes, in a way He did."

"What do you mean? Where did all this food come from?"

"I'll tell you in a minute, but first come wash up and let's have something to eat. Avremele already had his bottle and is sleeping peacefully, his tummy filled."

Naomi washed her hands, recited a *brachah,* and bit into the delicious sandwich filled with tuna, lettuce and tomatoes. "Tell me, Mommy, where did all this food come from?"

"Well," Mrs. Katz said, "While you were sleeping, news of our delay reached Antwerp."

"What's that?"

"Antwerp is a city. It has the largest Jewish population in Belgium."

"How far is it from here?"

"About forty-five minutes. When the Jews of Antwerp heard of

Flight to New York / 19

our situation, they immediately went into action and set up emergency food committees to bring us all this food quickly. They bought and prepared kosher food for all of the Jewish people stuck in the airport, and the volunteers put them in boxes and brought them to us as quickly as a speeding express."

Naomi looked around her. It was the middle of the night but it seemed like a big party was going on as four hundred hungry Jews ate and thanked *Hashem* for their good *mazel*.

Parents were calm. Children were laughing. Naomi bit into a juicy apple.

"There's so much food here we have enough to feed an army . . . maybe two armies."

"Mommy," Naomi wondered, "why did the Jews in Antwerp do this? They don't even know us and we don't know them. Why did they go to all this trouble for us? Why do they care about someone they don't even know?"

"I guess . . . it's because Jewish people feel like we all belong to one family."

"That's right. Like when we took our family trip to Arizona and we met that Jewish couple there. We never met them before yet we felt like we came from one family." Naomi drank some juice. "Why is that, Mommy?"

Mrs. Katz thought for a while. "Maybe," she said thoughtfully, "it's because all Jews were at *Har Sinai* when we received the Torah. There were millions of Jews standing around *Har Sinai* receiving the Torah, but we all felt so close to one another that we were like . . . one body with one heart."

"One body with one heart!" Naomi repeated. "You know Mommy, I feel close to the Jews in Antwerp and I don't even know them."

"Yes, I also feel a tremendous *hakaras hatov* for the *chesed* they showed us."

Naomi thought about this new discovery all the next day when the plane took off after a delay of twenty-seven hours.

"You're lucky," Naomi said to her doll Goldie. "You're lucky, because you belong to me and I belong to one big, beautiful family."

Mine Very Own Homon

It started out like any other ordinary normal Purim. We went to eat the *seudah* at Bubby's and Zeidy's like we do every year.

I was especially excited. I had my new costume. I had been saving for it for a year. I mowed lawns in the summer, raked leaves in the fall, and shoveled snow in the winter. And, now, finally I had the costume I always wanted. It looked authentic. It even scared me when I looked in the mirror. It was a costume of a real-life-looking gorilla. I loved it.

Nussy was dressed up as a Martian. Big deal! He painted his hands and face green and wore green pajamas. Everyone said how cute he looked, but even Bubby and Zeidy were impressed when I walked into the apartment.

"Oy, vey! You almost gave me de hot attack!" That was Bubby. She meant heart attack. That's how she speaks. Zeidy speaks the same way.

"Hilly, you tek off dat ugly monster soot."

"But, Bubby," I protested. "It's not a monster. It is a gorilla."

"A gorilla shmilla. Vun look at you und mine Homon landlord gonna trow you out."

Bubby and Zeidy have this thing about their landlord. He's pretty mean to them. I agree. He's always threatening to throw them out for every little thing. Actually I don't know why he doesn't. He could probably get more rent money from other people. But the truth is that he shouldn't complain. My grandpar-

ents should. His apartment house is so noisy every night. I think he's got a sewing machine factory down in the basement. You can hear the noise roaring till all hours of the night.

Anyway, Bubby and Zeidy call him their very own Homon. On Chanukah he complains when they light the *menorah*. Fire hazard! On Succos, he won't let them build a *succah*. Fire hazard! On Purim, he complains that there are too many people in their apartment. Fire hazard! I think he's got pyrophobia or something.

There's one thing Nussy and I love about Bubby's apartment. When we first saw it, Nussy asked, "What is that thing?" It was in the kitchen wall behind the kitchen shelves. "It looks like a secret panel in the wall," I said.

"That's the dumbwaiter," my mother explained. Nussy and I looked around.

"I don't see any waiter, dumb or smart," Nussy said.

"Neither do I."

My mother laughed. "Not a dumb waiter! A dumbwaiter! It was used years ago to move garbage from each floor down to the basement, or to bring groceries up from downstairs instead of carrying them up."

"Wow! Neato! Can we go in it?"

"No! Don't you dare!" My mother got that panicky look. "It's not meant for people, and besides, it hasn't been used for years. All that garbage going down attracts roaches. It's probably all rusty and broken."

"Why doesn't the landlord remove it?" I asked.

"Probably, it's too much trouble or, more likely, he's forgotten about it."

"Or maybe he doesn't even know about it," suggested Nussy.

In most of the apartments, the tenants keep things in front of the dumbwaiter so you don't even know it's there. But Nussy and I like to play with it. We move the kitchen shelves forward and I yell down to Nussy who answers me from the basement.

"Hellooo down there."

"Hellooo up there."

"Boys, vy you so noisy?" Bubby worried about her Homon again.

"Bubby, why don't you just tell him off one time," I said.

"Tell him off vat?" she was puzzled.

Zeidy was more hopeful. "Someday," he said, "He gonna go to jail. Dots vot I tink."

"To jail?" the thought thrilled me. "What for?"

"Maybe," said Zeidy, "for tax invasion." I didn't know what he meant.

It was Purim and we were sitting around the table. Uncle Ely and Aunt Dassy; my cousins, Tzvi and Ezra; Bubby and Zeidy, and the rest of us. Uncle Ely was singing up a storm. My father sang loudly. Tzvi and Ezra laughed and laughed.

After a while Nussy and I wandered off. I was still wearing my gorilla suit. To tell you the truth, I would have liked to take it off. It was hot and stuffy under it. But I paid a fortune for it and I was going to get my money's worth.

We walked into the kitchen. The counter was full of *shalach manos*, cakes, hamantashen, fruits, candy, soda cans.

"If I eat any more, I'm gonna bust," said Nussy.

"Me, too." Especially since it was so hard to eat through that gorilla mask.

Hilly and I must have thought about it at the same time. We were standing in front of the dumbwaiter. We looked at each other with unspoken agreement. We knew this was it. It was now or never.

"You first," said my brave brother. I'm a year older than he is.

"O.K." I was scared stiff.

I climbed in. The thing creaked. Nussy climbed in with me. It moved.

"Let's climb back out." It was too late.

The thing was really dumb. It started dragging us downward away from Bubby's kitchen. Thick darkness closed fast about us.

"Help!" We both yelled. But with all the noise going on in the dining room, our screams fell on deaf ears.

The thing kept pulling us farther and farther down. It creaked and it moaned. It was dark as night and the air was stale, musty and damp.

I was aware of the dampness in my palms and a throbbing pulse. I could hear Nussy whimpering.

"Is it gonna fall?"

"How should I know? This is my first ride too, y'know."

Then it stopped. I couldn't believe it. We were stuck somewhere between floors and we might stay here stuck in this stupid waiter forever.

My throat burned and was dry as the desert. My brain was hard at work but I couldn't come up with anything. Only down! I searched and groped.

Suddenly, I heard a faint familiar sound. Nussy heard it too.

"It's the sewing machines," he whispered.

"Oh, my jumping catfish! We must be in the landlord's apartment right in his kitchen behind his walls."

"Hurry up!" The shout was clear and fierce but it wasn't Nussy

Mine Very Own Homon / 27

who said it and it wasn't me. I stared at Nussy. Even though I couldn't see him, I could feel him shaking with fear.

That was our Homon landlord talking in his kitchen. If he knew we were in his walls, boy, would we be in for trouble! Real trouble! I took another breath. I couldn't seem to get enough air in my lungs.

"Hurry up!" The voice was near and clear. I thought for sure he could hear us breathing.

"Listen, I'm working as fast as I can!"

"Well, it's not good enough. We gotta finish this batch before midnight. The boss said we've got to get rid of this stuff by tomorrow."

I saw it first. A light shone through a crack. Nussy saw it too. We peeked in. We could see the whole kitchen.

What we saw nearly doubled us over; though we couldn't really double over any more than we already were.

Those sewing machines were not sewing machines. They weren't pouring out pants and shirts. They were pouring out crisp green dollar bills. Counterfeit money!

Our very own Homon was running a fake money factory right in his own home.

No wonder he didn't evict Bubby and Zeidy from their apartment. He figured an old couple would never discover his secret. Well, too bad for you, I thought. Your fun's over, Mister. We know about it now. Yeah! But what were we going to do about it?

Our predicament wasn't very funny either. Here we were stuck in this dumb waiter behind the walls. We couldn't move. Even if we could, we certainly couldn't stop those two criminals by ourselves.

Nussy must have been thinking the same thoughts. He shrugged his shoulders and lifted his arms in a gesture of despair. And that did it!

The next few minutes happened so fast, I can hardly recall every detail. When Nussy lifted his arm he must have pushed something. The wall fell open. A shelf fell down and there we were in the brightly lit room of our very own Homon.

My brain was in a tailspin. I drew a deep breath to steady myself. We were so scared we couldn't move. Neither could they.

They stared at us as if we were ghosts. Their eyes were so big I could only see a little black dot in the whites. They kept widening their eyes as if to focus them. They looked from me to Nussy. Me, in my gorilla costume, Nussy, all green and grimy.

One of them gulped, then made a dash for the door to escape. The other one followed.

They bumped into each other. One fell and hit his head on the table. He was out cold. The other ran so fast I thought he could win a marathon.

Nussy and I didn't waste any time either. We ran up the three flights of stairs to Bubby's apartment. We burst in. Nobody had missed us.

"Bubby! Zeidy!" We yelled. "Homon! Downstairs!"

It took a while, but we finally got our story out. The police were called, the scoundrels were arrested and I had my picture in the paper. Only it wasn't a picture of my face. It was a picture of a silly looking gorilla staring out.

And the headlines read:

GORILLA AND MARTIAN
OUTSMART A PRESENT-DAY HOMON

The Wild Stallion

I never wanted to go in the first place! But both my parents thought it would be "good" for me.

My uncle Danny said a month on the farm might be "just what I needed." Just what I needed! Ha! What I needed was for everyone to leave me alone.

"Don't slam the door!"

"Don't forget to do your homework!"

"Don't throw your clothes on the floor!" On and on and on!

"Is that you, Danny?" my aunt Helen called. I slammed the screen door hard.

"Who else can it be?" I yelled and shut myself up in the back room, where I slept.

"Danny, we'll be eating lunch in a few minutes."

"I don't want any," I answered loudly.

"Danny, please!" my Aunt Helen pleaded.

I felt sorry for her. I really didn't mean to make things so hard for them. It's just that I was mad. Good, fighting mad.

I felt my anger welling up inside me like a dark storm over the hayfields. I picked up my book and threw it across the room. I enjoyed hearing the crash as it hit the dresser.

I'm not sure why I was so mad and I don't know why I was always fighting and throwing my things around, and why I was always running, and running into trouble.

"Maybe he just has too much energy," I once heard my mother tell my father.

"Energy can be a good thing!" my father answered.

I thought about that. Would I always be so wild? I threw myself on the bed.

I thought about my uncle Danny's wild horses. That was the only nice part about being on the farm. I love animals, all kinds — dogs, cats, horses, lions, tigers. I used to have a pet parakeet, but my parents took it away from me because I didn't take good care of it.

I must have fallen asleep because the next thing I heard was loud shouting coming from outside. I rushed out. A large bay stallion was pawing at the ground. Uncle Danny and his men were frantically trying to get a rope around the young stallion. It was the wildest looking horse I have ever seen.

"Careful, men!" Uncle Danny shouted.

The horse reared, and bucked, and twisted his body into the air. I could see his wild eyes, his flaring nostrils, and flattened ears. He was enormous and scary looking. Would they ever be able to break such a wild beast and then ride him?

"Sam, you stand on this side. . . Dave on the other. . . Not too close now! That's it! Careful! Slow and easy. Slow and easy."

The stallion rolled his eyes wildly and his mane was whipping the air. It took the better part of an hour before the men managed to get a rope on him.

Uncle Danny came closer and closer and put a halter on him. Finally he was backed into the stall and the bar was dropped into place. Everyone was exhausted.

"Uncle Danny! Uncle Danny!" I yelled. "Do you think you'll ever tame him? He's so big and wild! I've never seen such a horse before!"

Uncle Danny and I walked back to the house together. "When

you train an animal," he said, "you have to train him very slowly. It doesn't happen overnight, but I think in good time, he'll be trained like the other horses."

That evening, at supper, I couldn't stop talking about the stallion.

"Uncle Danny, can I name him?" I asked excitedly.

Uncle Danny lifted his fork to his mouth and looked at me. "Yes," he said.

"I want to name him 'Prince.'"

"Fine with me!"

Prince! He was Prince of the Horses. A wild prince now, but maybe soon, a gentle and good prince.

"Uncle Danny," I repeated. "Do you think he'll ever be trained? He's so wild!"

Uncle Danny finished eating before he spoke in his slow fashion.

"The lion is the king of the animals, fierce and terrible. All the other animals tremble at his roar because they know he has strong teeth and powerful jaws. Yet, it is possible to train a lion to be so gentle that you can put your arms around it."

"Like in the circus?" I asked.

"That's right!"

"Last year I went to an aqua show. I saw a trained seal catch fish and throw them back to the keeper. I couldn't believe it! Why didn't the seal eat the fish?"

"Because the seal was trained, Danny. It learned to curb its own desires, to control its own will."

"Just like people," I muttered. I wondered if I could ever be trained not to lose my temper and not to fight all the time.

Aunt Helen cleared the table. "It's harder for people," she said, "because *Hashem* gave people free choice."

The Wild Stallion / 33

"I know that! It means *Hashem* wants people to be able to *choose* right from wrong. Otherwise, he would have made everybody be good all the time."

But I was uneasy. Could I ever be "trained?" Could I be weaned from my bad temper, like the stallion in the stall?

The next morning I jumped out of bed and scrambled into my clothes. I hurried to the stable near the barn. A hawk soared in circles, and a cow stood quietly in the meadow. I opened the stall door and walked in gingerly. Prince was quiet. "Is he asleep?" I wondered.

From up close he loomed even larger than yesterday. He was a giant horse, fierce and terrible. "Like me," I thought.

"Hi, Prince!" I said gently. "I'd like to be your friend."

Prince snorted and shied away. I took a brush from a nail and went closer to brush his coat.

Prince threw his head back, whinnied, and lunged forward.

My eyes were blinded by a cloud of dust as I stood, paralyzed with fear. The thundering hooves towered above me and I could feel the horse's hot breath on my cheek.

I couldn't cry, I couldn't shout. I stood with my feet rooted to the ground. Then, suddenly, I felt myself lifted.

"Are you crazy?" I heard one of Uncle Danny's workers say as he whisked me away. "What were you trying to do?"

"I . . . I . . . wanted to brush his coat," I stammered.

"You can't get close to him until he's been broken! Don't you know that? You could have been killed!"

I was shaking like a leaf and went slowly to my room.

During the next few weeks, I watched from a distance, as Uncle Danny and his men tried to tame the wildness in Prince.

Day after day, I watched as the men took turns riding him.

Prince put his head down and began to double back, jumping up in the air like a goat, hitting the ground and then leaping again, throwing each rider to the ground.

He ran around the corral with wild abandon. I felt I understood him. I pulled a blade of grass and slid it between my teeth. The trees were casting long shadows and the sun was slipping behind the hills.

"Come on, Prince!" I whispered. "Calm down and be good! If a lion can do it, you can do it."

Every day I cleaned the stall and put down fresh straw and feed and refilled the water bucket.

It took a long time, but the day finally came when Prince allowed the men to ride him.

One day, at the end of the summer, I took a long broom and a bucket of water and washed the walls of Prince's stall. Then I walked out to the pasture.

"Here, Prince, come!" I said. The horse pranced towards me, his head held high.

He took the carrot from my hand. After that we became friends. Sometimes I brought him a lump of sugar, sometimes an apple. Prince seemed to enjoy the feel of my hand on his neck and the sound of my voice.

"You know, Prince," I said, stroking his back. "You used to be wild as the wind and now you're so gentle and tame."

Prince looked at me with his enormous brown eyes. "And if you can do it," I said suddenly, "then so can I. If a wild horse's nature can be changed and he can be gentled, then I, too, can train myself to break a bad habit, like my quick temper.

"It won't happen overnight, like Uncle Danny says, but if I start now, that day might come sooner than I expect."

The Skunk Hero

Being the middle kid of six brothers and one sister is no picnic, let me tell you! Especially if everyone is so "special" in something and all I'm special in is being the middle child.

Eli is fifteen and, boy! Is he smart! He's away in *Yeshivah* and he already finished half of all the *Mishnayos* in *Shaas*.

Heshy was just *bar mitzvah* and he sings like a bird, his voice sweet and strong. He's learning to be a *baal kriah* so that he can read the *Torah* in *shul* every *Shabbos*. He's already been the *chazzan* many times.

Josh is eleven. He and I fight constantly. That's because we both want to go to camp this summer and only one of us can go. It seems only right that if Josh went last summer it is my turn to go this summer.

Then comes me. Shully, the middle kid! The no-hero kid! I'll be ten on *Chanukah*.

Malky is a year younger than me and of course she gets so much attention because she's the only girl in the family.

"Stay out of my room, Monkey Face!" she says to me.

"Don't call me Monkey Face, you . . . you . . ." I couldn't say it. Not that I couldn't think of any names! "Skinny" or "Smarty" would fit, but I just couldn't call her names and hurt her feelings.

I just can't do things like that, and besides, I probably do look like a monkey. I'm small for my age. People think I'm six, but I'll be ten on Chanukah. I'm dark and my eyes are set close. My mother says I'm cute but all mothers think their kids are cute.

Pesach is six and he really is cute with his missing front teeth and big sunny smile.

Pinny is the baby so, of course, all he has to do is give his toothy grin and say anything and everybody acts like he is a genius.

My dad is an accountant. That means he helps people figure out how to handle their money. I wish he'd figure out how to handle our money. Then, maybe Josh and I could both go to camp.

My mom used to be a teacher. Now she says she has enough teaching at home with us kids keeping her busy twenty-four hours a day. I tell her that she would have an easier summer if I were away at camp.

"All my friends are going to camp," Josh always says. "Why do you want to go?"

" 'Cause I've never been to camp. That's why. And you already went."

"But you can go another year. Your friends are all going to be here, but I'll have nothing to do without any of my friends here."

But my dad has a different system. We've got to earn our keep and the way we earn it is by doing well in school. He doesn't care about *grades* and stuff like that! All he wants is to see us work and try hard.

Well, I used to fool around in school pretty much and I'd forget to do my homework, so Josh was usually winning, but lately I'm trying harder. I read a two-hundred-page book and made a five-page book report on it, and I learned to read *Chumash* with *Rashi* with almost no mistakes.

≈ ≈ ≈

Lots of times I dream of being a hero, and doing something like saving someone from drowning, except there aren't too many people drowning in my neighborhood these days.

Maybe some day the dreams that are in my head and the things that happen to me outside of my head will come together and I'll be a real hero.

This past summer we spent a week at my Uncle Nachi's bungalow in the country. I helped in the day camp with the kindergarten kids. I liked it and I think the kids liked me. At least, nobody called me any names.

"Lunch time" the counselor announced, "We've got two kinds of sandwiches, peanut butter and sardines. Who wants peanut butter?"

"Me!" Eleven little boys raised their hands.

"Who wants sardines?" One boy raised his hand meekly. Everybody laughed. I felt so sorry for him. Sardines are not my favorite food either, but I sure felt bad for this kid with everyone laughing at him.

"I'll take a sardine sandwich, too," I said, and suddenly all laughter stopped.

That was the summer I got my new nickname. It happened when my Dad was having a meeting with his new boss, Mr. Sanders, at the bungalow. If Mr. Sanders would agree, Dad would get a promotion. That means, getting a better job in the job you already have or something like that. Anyway, it was important to Dad so he shooed us "little kids" away. I was included, as if I were a little kid, and I'm nine and three-quarters and becoming ten on *Chanukah*.

I climbed a tall chestnut tree and curled myself into a tight ball. A squirrel scampered up a nearby tree. White clouds were whipping across the sky like sailboats. I could hear the wind in the trees, rustling the leaves. Bees buzzed and birds were calling to each other over the trees. A cricket chirped and frogs croaked in a nearby creek. Mmmm . . . ahhh . . . The air was fresh and smelled of growing things and damp earth.

    The whole day lay ahead of me with boundless opportunities. I began my usual daydreams of being a hero. Maybe I could think of a way to help Dad get his promotion. Then, not only would I be a hero but I'd probably get to go to camp too.

    "Let me explain my ideas to you, Mr. Sanders."

    Uh Oh! It was Dad and Mr. Sanders. They were coming out of the cottage right towards the tree that I was sitting in.

    Now they were right under me. If I called out to them I might disturb them and ruin Dad's promotion. So I decided to keep quiet and stay put.

    "You've got some fine ideas, Mr. Lando. Let me hear some more."

    They kept up a steady flow of talk. I got tireder and tireder.

    Suddenly the branch creaked and groaned under me. A ripple of panic ran through me. There was a lump in my throat. My heart lurched in terror. I could feel the hair on the back of my neck stand straight up as the branch got weaker and weaker and began to creak louder.

    "Mr. Lando, I think you are . . ." The words caught in his throat as I fell right on top of Mr. Sanders. He stopped my fall and the wet earth stopped his fall.

    I stood up quickly. My father shook his head as if spiders had spun some kind of web around him. I think I was too stunned to cry and I couldn't move for a second. Then I jumped to my feet and ran off into the woods, quick as a cat after a bird.

I was so scared. What a goof I was! But if I thought I was finished being a goof, I was wrong.

I ran like a rabbit and tripped over a black rock, or what I thought was a black rock.

"Yikes!" That was no rock. That was an honest-to-goodness black and white skunk.

The skunk frightened by my appearance, defended itself by doing what skunks do. I escaped one way, the skunk the other. I ran with the smell of skunk bringing tears to my eyes and making me choke and gag.

Oy gevalt! It took twenty baths of tomato juice before I was able to be in the same room with others without their twitching their noses at me. With all that tomato juice I almost began thinking like a pizza.

Anyway, Dad did get his promotion, no thanks to me, and I got a new nickname, "The Skunk Hero," which wasn't the kind of hero I wanted to be.

Well, this year I decided it was going to be different. I worked really hard in school.

So today was to be the big day. Dad was going to announce the "winner" right before our trip to Chicago.

My cousin, Breina, was getting married and we were all going to the *chasunah* in our '72 station wagon.

Mom and Dad and all of us were loading the car.

"Dad," I said, "can you tell us now?"

"No, Shully." Dad was firm. "We've got to finish packing up first." I worked hard. I carried suitcases, bags of food, my books, games and diapers.

The car looked like it couldn't hold another ounce.

"Oh, No!" Mom exclaimed, "I almost forgot Cholent." Dad

moaned. "Cholent" is a stuffed animal that Pinchas takes with him wherever he goes; it's twice as big as he is. "Do we have to take that monstrous thing with us?"

Right before the journey we all went to wash up and change our clothes.

"O.K. Shully, Josh." Dad called us. Now was the moment. Would I be the lucky one? Would Dad choose me to go to camp?

Josh and I stood alone in the kitchen with Dad and Mom.

"I spoke to both your *Rebbes* last night," Dad said, "and it seems you both have been working very hard and doing very good work. You've become organized, responsible and shown maturity. I'm very proud of both of you." He stopped. So did my heart.

"Mom and I decided that since you are tied, it would be only fair to let you, Shully, go since you, Josh, went last year!"

I couldn't believe it. Finally! Happiness swelled up inside me . . . till I turned and looked at Josh.

He had a miserable, sorrowful look on his face but he didn't say a word. He just walked out of the kitchen slowly, his shoulders drooping, his head down.

When he was gone, I swallowed hard. "Dad," I said, "I . . . um . . . I don't think I really want to go to camp this year."

"What?!"

"Well, it's just that I really could go another year. My friends are all here. Josh's friends will all be going this year and he wants to go so badly. I still have my friends, and you, and Mom, and my goldfish, Knaidel. I guess I could go next year if it's okay with you."

Dad's eyes were warm with approval and made me feel ten feet tall. Mom rushed over to me and squeezed me hard.

"Why'd you do that?" I asked.

She laughed. "You're the goodest, kindest *yingele* I've ever squeezed."

I felt good. Maybe I wasn't a famous hero. Maybe I was just a quiet hero who nobody knows is a hero except me, and of course, *Hashem,* and I think that's the best kind of hero that a person could be.

"Come on, let's go!" Everyone shouted from the car. Hershel and Josh and Malky and Pesach and Pinny were all packed into the car. Eli was away at *yeshivah.*

Dad and Mom got into the front seat. I stood near the car and looked at my family packed in like sardines. It reminded me of last summer's lunch.

Here we go again, I thought. There was no room for me, the middle kid.

Mom opened the front car door. "Squeeze in, Sugar-plum." I laughed. I squeezed myself in the front between Mom and Dad.

Dad punched me affectionately. If was cozy in the front seat, in the middle, squashed between Mom on one side, and Dad on the other.

You know, sometimes, being in the middle isn't so bad.

Go Ahead and Shoot Me

"ive up or we'll shoot you!"

"No, never, never!"

"Then we must throw you into the fire."

"You can throw me into the fire. You can throw me into the ocean. You can shoot me! You can tie me to a tree and starve me! You can throw me into jail! But I'll never give up my religion. I'll always remain a Jew!"

BANG!

"Excuse me! This is my stop!"

"Oh, I'm sorry," Chaya Malka stood up and let the woman move out to get off the bus. She moved closer to the window and continued daydreaming.

Avraham *Avinu* was ready to sacrifice his only son to *Hashem*. Years later, another Avraham, Avraham Ben Avraham, gave up his life, rather than give up his Jewishness. All those *Yidden* through the ages who died rather than give up living as Jews!

All the *Yidden* through the ages who were killed in the war simply because they were Jews. All the *Yidden* throughout history who died *Al Kiddush Hashem* rather than give up being Jewish.

Chaya Malka felt that she wanted to make a *Kiddush Hashem*. Maybe she could . . . Naw! She was too young for that.

Maybe someday she would . . . Naw! She didn't know how to do that.

Maybe . . . No, no, it would never work.

Thump! Chaya Malka fell to the floor with a loud bump.

"Move it, kid!"

It was that tall, freckled girl who came on the bus everyday with her gang of friends.

"That was my seat!" Chaya Malka said angrily.

"Oh, it was! Was it?" said the tall girl. "I don't see your name written on it!"

The other girls laughed, piercing the air with their wild shrieks. Chaya Malka could see the bus driver looking at them in his rearview mirror. She got up and walked away. The girls poked one another and roared.

One girl bumped into Chaya Malka, causing her books to drop. Chaya Malka's forehead wrinkled beneath her dark bangs as she bent down and quickly picked them up.

What a bunch of show-offs. Couldn't they see how awful they looked?

Everyone was staring at them. Some had frowns on their faces. Some just shook their heads. Chaya Malka moved towards the back of the bus, away from the girls.

> They followed her up the twisting steep hill.
>
> "Chaya Malka, this is your last chance! Do you hear us?"
>
> "Yes, I hear you!"
>
> "Do you understand?"
>
> "Yes, I understand." She stuffed her knuckles into her mouth to stop the scream that was rising rapidly in her throat.
>
> Her eyes were blindfolded, her hands were tied behind her back. Her palms felt clammy and her stomach was tied in a tight ball.
>
> A large crowd gathered below, watching. The whole city seemed to be there. Reporters were writing furiously in their notepads. Photographers were trying to get closer. Old men shook their heads, admiringly.

Mothers wiped their tears. Children stared with their mouths open.

"Chaya Malka, what is your answer?"

Chaya Malka lifted her head proudly. "My answer now and always will be the same. No! No! I will never do as you say. I will always remain a Jew. You can kill my body, but you can never kill my neshamah. I am a Jew now and forever!"

The crowd roared. "She is so brave."

"She is so strong."

"Incredible."

"Amazing!"

"What a Kiddush Hashem!" . . .

Plunk!

The bus jerked to a stop and Chaya Malka fell against the window, her dreams still clinging to her like cobwebs.

"Bye, Chaya Malka!" Her friends were getting off at their usual stop.

"Bye, Shoshana. Bye, Suri. See you tomorrow!"

"Goodbye, Mr. Harris." The girls waved to the bus driver. "Thank you."

He smiled back, "Goodbye, girls."

Chaya Malka continued to stare out the window, but she didn't see the street, the stores, the people rushing by. Her thoughts were far away.

"Hey, you — move over."

She was jarred out of her dreams again by the same tall, freckled girl.

Why are those girls always making trouble? I wish they'd leave me alone, she thought. She huddled deeper into the corner seat to keep her distance from the rowdy bunch.

"You dope!"

The raucous laughter chilled her. But this time the words were not addressed to her. Chaya Malka's eyes opened wide as she realized that the girls were picking on one of their own this time. They were pushing the tall, freckled girl. Her books flew all over the bus.

The gang of girls hooted with laughter and got off the bus, leaving the tall girl furious. She began picking up her possessions.

Quarters and dimes rolled, pencils and papers flew up and down the bus floor as the bus moved on.

Before she realized what she was doing, Chaya Malka was on her hands and knees helping. She picked up the change, books and papers, and handed them to the girl. The bus driver watched from the front mirror. The tall, freckled girl kept her eyes down.

"Thanks," she mumbled.

She quickly got off the bus, her face flushed and confused looking.

At the next stop, Chaya Malka moved down the aisle to the front of the bus. It was her stop. The bus driver smiled at her.

'You're one of the girls who goes to that Hebrew School on Park Heights Avenue, aren't you?"

"Yes," she answered.

He nodded. "I can tell."

Chaya Malka got off the bus.

Suddenly her dreams seemed to have come to real life. She had made a *Kiddush Hashem*, hadn't she? *Kiddush Hashem* doesn't only mean dying for *Hashem*. It means living for *Hashem*.

She would be a living *Kiddush Hashem* every day! Every minute! With her speech, with her walk, and with her dress! She

would show the world how the children of the King act.

> Chaya Malka could see a crowd of people around her home speaking to her mother. She recognized some of the faces. The janitor from school . . . the cashier from the supermarket . . . the bus driver . . .
>
> "Your daughter is always so kind and polite . . . so respectful . . . your daughter carried my packages up to my door . . . your daughter always greets me with a smile . . . your daughter . . ."

Chaya Malka bumped into a tree and didn't hear the rest.

The Old Man

He was old. But not so old that he couldn't still teach. He loved children and children loved him.

"I'm sorry, Reb Chatzkel, but we just don't have the money to hire another teacher."

He heard these words over and over. He tried applying for other kinds of jobs too, but what could an old man do? He had been a teacher all his life. How could he start working at something that he had never done before?

He pushed his wire-rimmed glasses up on his thin nose. "*Hashem* will help," he said. His savings were almost used up. He sold some of his furniture and moved into a smaller apartment. But still, time and money were running short.

His children wanted to help him. They offered him money. They offered him a place to live. But he was a proud old man. All his life he had been independent. He had always taken care of himself and he wanted to continue to take care of himself.

"I appreciate your desire to help," he told the children, as he gently but firmly refused their offers.

The children, all grown with families of their own, were concerned. What should they do? They loved their father. They wanted to help him. They wanted him to do what he loved best — to teach. But what could they do?

One little grandson studied with Reb Chatzkel every night. He was a quiet boy with large mournful eyes. The old man loved his grandson very much. The little boy loved his grandfather.

The Old Man / 51

They sat in the small crowded kitchen, a small lamp on the round table, and boy and man learned the sweet words of the *Torah* together.

It was the highlight of the old man's day. For him the sun never set as long as he was teaching *Torah*.

When they were through, the two would sit and talk. The little boy ate crackers and drank milk and told his grandfather about his day in *yeshivah*. The old man sipped his hot tea slowly and told his grandson stories of his youth.

Time passed and still Reb Chatzkel could not find a job. The little boy saw the sadness in the old man's eyes. It hurt him. He put his arms around Reb Chatzkel's neck and laid his small head against the steady thump of the old man's heart.

There must be something they could do to help him. He thought about it every night in bed. He thought about it when he *davened*.

One day, he had an idea. He spoke about it with his parents. They called his aunts and uncles to a meeting. The little boy told them his plan. They discussed it, and everyone thought it was a wonderful idea.

The little boy's father approached a *yeshivah*. "My father is an old man," he said. "He has been a teacher all his life, and he is still an excellent teacher. But he cannot find a teaching job now."

The *yeshivah* principal listened with sympathy. "I understand," he said. Reb Chatzkel had already approached him and he wanted to help.

The little boy's father continued. "I know the *yeshivah* does not have enough money to hire an additional teacher. But my family has a suggestion." He explained his son's idea to the principal. The principal thought it was a good idea, too, so Reb Chatzkel was given a job teaching a small group of students in the *yeshivah*.

He was now a happy old man doing what he loved best in the world, teaching *Torah* to little boys.

Every week the family paid money to the *yeshivah*, and every week the *yeshivah* paid that money to Reb Chatzkel.

And the happiest of all was the little boy who loved his grandfather . . . the old man.

Opening Night

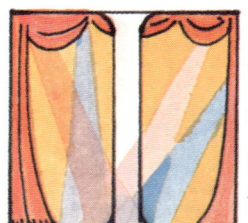I could never do it. That's for sure. I mean, to get up in front of five hundred people and sing a song all by myself. Just the thought gives me the shudders. I get panicky even when I get up in front of the class to give a book report.

"Just relax," my best friend, Shifra, tells me. She's the one who is going to sing the solo. It's easy for her to say. She loves getting up on stage and performing.

Ever since we were little, Shifra was always the talented performer and I was the talented cheerer from the audience. I clapped and cheered and yelled for my best friend. But I also breathed a sigh of relief. She was on the stage and I was in my cozy, secure seat in the audience.

"You've got to try out for concert," Shifra begged me for the twentieth time.

"I told you a million times, NO! You should know better than to keep asking me."

"But you've got such a beautiful voice," Shifra insisted.

She's right. I do sing pretty nicely, especially with Shifra. Our voices blend beautifully and we harmonize lots of songs, but privately, in my room. Never in front of an audience.

"Oh, I give up on you," Shifra had said.

Thank goodness! Now I would have peace from her nagging and enjoy the concert rehearsals.

I loved watching them practice. To tell you the truth, I secretly admired all those girls up there on the stage, singing up a storm.

Opening Night / 55

I love music and singing. If I weren't so shy and scared I'd be up there with those girls singing to my heart's content too.

I watched Shifra standing so confidently, with poise, her voice rich and clear. I knew all the songs by heart, with every bit of harmony.

While they sang up on stage I sang softly to myself in my seat. I didn't miss one practice session.

"You know," said Kaila, the head of concert, "considering the amount of time you spend here . . ."

"I know, I know," I finished for her, "I might as well be up there singing." She smiled at me but left me alone.

On opening night I felt as nervous as if I were going to be up on stage. Shifra was her usual calm self.

"Aren't you even a little nervous?" I asked.

"What for?" She didn't even know what I meant.

The hall was filled to capacity. Girls were clustered around the stage. I looked around from the front seat Shifra had reserved for me. I saw my teachers, friends, neighbors and people I never met. The entire school was there for opening night. Out of the sea of faces, I saw my mother waving to me. I waved back.

The air was full of excitement, noise and bustle. Mrs. Sidell, the pianist, sat very straight, her hands poised above the keyboard.

Suddenly, the lights went out and people rushed to their seats. A hush fell over the audience as the music began. I felt shivers run up my spine. The band started playing and the curtains opened slowly.

There was a roar of applause. I saw the smiling happy faces of the girls across the footlights. I looked at Shifra. She looked happy and composed.

I sang along with the girls. Cheer and applause greeted every song. I loved it.

I waited eagerly for Shira's solo. Now it was coming. MAH RABU MAASECHA HASHEM! How Great Are Your Deeds, *Hashem!*

Shifra approached the microphone. She looked straight at the audience and smiled brightly. The keyboard sounded the introduction to her song. Slowly . . . melodious . . . now! MAH RABU MAASECHA HASHEM!

My face froze. Shifra didn't look right. She kept twisting a strand of her long dark hair around her finger. She looked stunned. She was staring blankly at the audience. Her smile was gone and she wasn't singing.

MAH RABU MAASECHA HASHEM! I practically screamed from my seat. Shifra mouthed the words but no sound came out. The music stopped. Then slowly it began again. I slumped in my chair. The sound of the piano seemed to buzz in my head like a swarm of homeless bees.

"Sing, Shifra, sing." I almost choked on the words. But Shifra just stood there as if mesmerized. She looked like a frozen statue. She blinked and then just stared with her mouth slightly open.

Again, for the third time now the introduction to her song began. You could hear the restless shuffling in the audience.

Suddenly, someone jumped up from her seat and rushed up onto the stage. She was standing beside Shifra. I heard her begin singing Shifra's song. MAH RABU MAASECHA HASHEM!

The voice was mine! I was up there on stage standing next to my best friend, singing her solo. My mouth was dry and my legs began to shake.

This seemed to wake Shifra out of her stupor. She opened her mouth and sang along with me. The audience must have thought that that was why she hadn't begun singing. She had been waiting for me, her partner.

We sang together with harmony. In a haze of disbelief, I felt like we were in my room at home and I gave it all I had. Shifra seemed to be singing better than usual too, realizing what an amazing thing was happening.

I still can't believe it. There I was, Yocheved Rus, the girl who doesn't open her mouth in front of anyone, singing with her best friend in front of five hundred people! Will wonders never cease?

And you know what? I loved it! The audience loved it, too. I heard an explosion of applause and they gave us a standing ovation. I found myself wiping my eyes with my sleeves.

Shifra was great for the rest of the performance and I settled back into my front seat.

I don't know whether this first time will be my last time. All I know is that I felt a close bond with my best friend. And when Shifra smiled at me from the stage, I knew that if I had to do it again, I would.

Dov Dov and the Big Potch

It was going to be a great party! Dov Dov finished writing his list. Chaim Newman, . . . Sruly Shane, Mendy Blumberg.

The list included twenty boys, all of Dov Dov's best friends. "We're going to have great fun," Dov Dov told Yossi walking home from school.

"What are we going to do?" Yossi asked.

"First, we'll eat, of course," said Dov Dov. "My dad is going to make hot dogs for us on our grill in the back yard."

"Mmmm, yum!"

"Then my dad is going to tell us a story. You should hear his stories!"

"That's great! And then?"

"And then we'll all go into the yard and play all sorts of games. I have some great prizes too."

Dov Dov was excited. He had never had a birthday party before. This year his parents agreed to let him have one. He had been planning the party for weeks. The only thing left to do was to mail out the invitations.

"Yossi, will you help me write out the invitations?"

"Sure, I have nothing else to do."

"Well, look who's here, Baby Birthday Boy!"

Dov Dov looked up to see Potch Cooperstein, a big stocky boy, blocking his way.

"Excuse me," Dov Dov spoke angrily. "You're in my way."

"Oh! I'm sorry," Potch said loudly. He looked at Dov Dov as if he were something that had crawled out from under a rock. "We wouldn't want to get in the way of the Birthday Baby, would we?" He laughed. So did the three boys who were with him.

Resentment rose in Dov Dov like a scalding wave. "Potch, why don't you leave me alone already," said Dov Dov.

"Sure," said Potch. His lips curled into an unpleasant grin. "I'll leave you alone. That's exactly what you deserve to be, alone."

"Potch why are you so mean to me? What did I ever do to you anyway?"

"Do? You? You could never do anything to me, Dov Dov. I just like you, that's all. This is how I treat people I like." He gave Dov Dov a push. Dov Dov lost his balance and fell on his back. Potch and his buddies laughed and ran away.

"Dov Dov, are you all right?" asked Yossi.

"Yeah, I'm okay." He got up and brushed himself off. His whole body bristled with anger. Yossi picked up his paper.

"Boy, I sure wish I could have just one chance to get even with that Potch Cooperstein. I'd show him what a big bully he is."

"Come on, Dov Dov," Yossi said, trying to change the subject, "let's go to your house and finish the invitations."

Dov Dov grudgingly agreed. By the time the boys reached his house he was in a good mood again.

"Hershel Dinowitz lives on Winner, doesn't he?" asked Yossi trying to write neatly.

"Yep."

"Where does Peretz Cohen live?"

"4902 Greenspring Avenue," answered Dov Dov.

"Dov Dov, can I just write the initials of the boys on the envelope? It would save a lot of time."

"Sure, I don't mind. I appreciate your helping me, Yossi."

"I could mail these for you on the way home if you want me to!"

"Thanks, Yossi."

Dov Dov could hardly wait. The day was coming closer.

"I got your invitation, Dov Dov," said Hershel Dinowitz.

"My parents said I could come. Thanks for inviting me."

"Me, too," said Mendy Blumberg. How exciting! All his good friends were coming.

Only Peretz Cohen hadn't answered. Dov Dov called him on the phone. No answer. Dov Dov let the phone ring for a long time. There was still no answer.

Peretz was one of Dov Dov's best friends. Well, thought Dov Dov, if he can't come he must have a good reason.

The day of the party arrived. "Hi, Dov Dov, Happy Birthday." Dov Dov smiled with delight. He had been looking forward to this day for a long time.

The room was full of many laughing boys crowding around the table.

The door opened suddenly and a hush fell on the room. There stood Potch Cooperstein. He looked around the room. All the boys stared at him.

"Oh, bumblesticks!" hissed Dov Dov. "What's he doing here? He'd better not try to spoil my party."

The boys had their eyes glued to Dov Dov as he approached Potch. The feeling in the air was uncertain and menacing.

Dov Dov mustered all the courage he could and neared Potch. He was about to open his mouth when Potch smiled shyly.

"Happy Birthday, Dov Dov. Thank you for inviting me."

Dov Dov's forehead wrinkled in a frown. What was he talking about? He had never invited Potch.

Potch saw Dov Dov's puzzled face. "See, here, I got your

invitation." He handed Dov Dov a grimy envelope addressed to:

P.C.
4209 Greenspring Avenue

"Oh, no!" thought Dov Dov. "So that was why Peretz didn't come. That invitation was supposed to say 4902 Greenspring! Yossi must have made a mistake when he wrote the address. And Potch Cooperstein and Peretz Cohen both have the same initials."

Dov Dov still hadn't spoken. "It isn't a mistake, is it?" asked Potch. His face was an interesting shade of deep brick red.

Something scratched in the back of Dov Dov's brain and he couldn't quite remember what it was.

Yossi whispered into his ear, "You're not going to let him stay and spoil your party are you, Dov Dov?"

Of course not. This was his chance to show that Potch. As if he thought Dov Dov really wanted him at his party.

"Was it a mistake, Dov Dov?" Potch repeated in a small voice. His shoulders sagged.

Slowly, the stirring memory surfaced. Dov Dov knew what this scene reminded him of.

It was the story of Kamtza and Bar Kamtza. One was the friend and one the enemy. The enemy got invited to the party by mistake. His host threw him out and it was the last straw that brought about the destruction of the *Bais Hamikdash*.

Dov Dov fixed his eyes on Potch with a steady gaze.

"No, it wasn't a mistake," he said loudly. "Come in. The party is just beginning."

Potch's face lit up. He walked in awkwardly. Yossi stared, his mouth open.

A few boys shoved their way over to Dov Dov and started whispering anxiously. "Hey, Dov Dov, why'd you let him stay?"

Dov Dov took a glass of orange soda and held it high. His generous mouth broadened into a bright smile.

"*Lechaim!*" he said. Then he turned to Yossi and whispered, "I just brought the *Bais Hamikdash* a little closer to us."